HEART FAILED
IN THE BACK
OF A TAXI

HEART FAILED IN THE BACK OF A TAXI

POEMS

Pedram Navab

iUniverse LLC
Bloomington

HEART FAILED IN THE BACK OF A TAXI
POEMS

iUniverse books may be ordered through booksellers or by contacting:

iUniverse LLC
1663 Liberty Drive
Bloomington, IN 47403
www.iuniverse.com
1-800-Authors (1-800-288-4677)

ISBN: 978-1-4620-4679-9 (sc)
ISBN: 978-1-4620-4680-5 (e)

Printed in the United States of America

iUniverse rev. date: 05/05/2014

TO REY CHOW,
A PEERLESS MENTOR

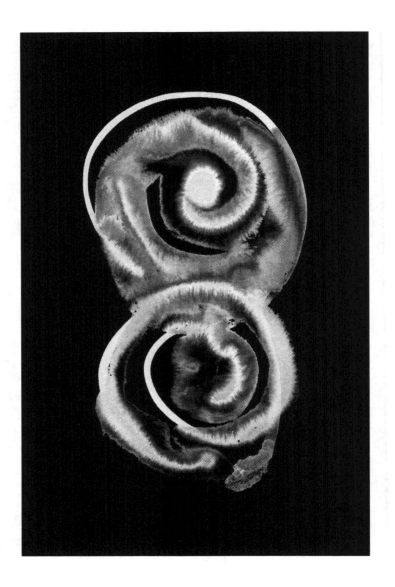

I wish I could eat your cancer when you turn black.

Kurt Cobain

Don't say *Mourning*. It's too psychoanalytic. I'm not *mourning*. I'm suffering.

Roland Barthes

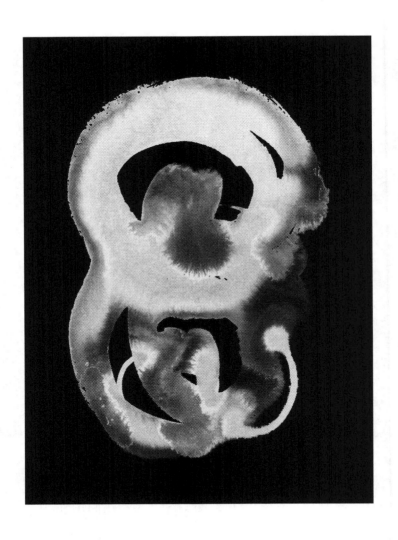

Dead hearts are everywhere.

Torquil Campbell

To love is *donner ce qu'on n'a pas,* to give what one does not have.

Miran Bozovic

Who has not sat before his own heart's curtain? it lifts: and the scenery is falling apart.

Rainer Maria Rilke

PART I:

AORTIC DISSECTIONS

Heartland

A succubus or a vampire
it doesn't matter anyway
she sucks the blood out of me
centrifuges it with her mouth
and spits out what she doesn't need,
what she doesn't want:
the plasma, the platelets

she keeps the reticulocytes
and plans to harvest them
so she doesn't have to suck on me
anymore

—You're getting old
she tells me
—Your blood won't be so good
—I have to get what I can
—Now
—And plan for the future

I look at her,
this demon,
this vampire,
this whatever,
and pity her for needing my blood
so bad
that she plans her life around
my reticulocytes

but she sucks the last drop out of me,
takes off one of her red Louboutin stiletto
pumps,
throws it at me as a memento and says
—You'll be doing your own sucking
—Again
—You bastard

For the first time, my bloodless black heart
beats for her

CORPSE POSE

Nineteen
tattoos
twenty
three
teeth
enucleated
right
eye
caput
medusae
hepato
spleno
megaly
sagging
jaundiced
skin
thinning
hair
amputation
below
the
left
knee
six
bullets
in
the
heart

Xanax

The vulnerable scream of the telephone,
3:59 am

It's too late for any good news,
early enough for what he
expects

The hyenas and wolves outside
compete with the telephone's
cry

Their ears are steadfast and propped
They command him:
—Answer it now
—Answer the telephone

The howling outside continues
The full moon listens in
The owl's head is fixed
The longcase clock strikes 4
The hyena robs a grave

He doesn't need to answer

THE FOREIGNER[*]

The foreigner
cocoons herself in numbed skin
and hardens her emancipated body
and loses herself in the
strangers, the
crowds,
herself

She likes it this way

New tongue,
she speaks but does not truly
understand
She throws herself in deeply,
all of herself

Here,
she can be the ruthless and kinky
lover that she could never be in her
chador,
her burka,
her niqab

[*] "Poem was inspired by Julia Kristeva's *"Strangers to Ourselves"*"

She has been here two years now
Her herpes sore is markedly
visible on her lips
Her cervix has been biopsied for
cancer
She has contracted hepatitis C from a tattoo
design etched with
a non-sterilized needle

But she has been the
happiest that she has ever been
as the foreigner within the foreigners
as the stranger in the crowd
as the lover with no shame

She brushes her dyed midnight green and
vermilion
red hair away from her eyes
and glimpses
the needle track marks on her
left arm
and smiles
as she awaits the results of her
HIV test

She has never been happier,
the foreigner

DAMAGES

Like a dead Greek,
shrouded
in white,
ensconced
in his coffin

He is unperfected,
a damaged Perseus,
trauma
to
the
head, neck

a Grecian urn,
broken,
the reddish clay of the vase,
split,
the painted manlike gods,
emasculated, downcast

He awakens:
a group of celestial
men,
donned in white
The unbearable lightness
pierces, blinds him
momentarily

He remembers the deadly
quicksand of the Rub'al-Khali,
he remembers the militia

In heaven,
at last
The blow to the
head, neck
deliverance from an
unjust, cruel world

Until he hears the
cacophony of the
MRI
scanner
and smells
the medicinal
aura of the hospital
and cannot move
his arms and legs anymore

Somewhere,
Medusa
laughs

LOST & FOUND

We lost him in the fire
—our Grandfather
along with the fake Van Gogh painting
(Portrait of an Old Man with Beard)
that we purchased at the flea market

He couldn't come down the stairs
fast enough
—our Grandfather
and he lost time
with his shuffling gait and tremors
while trying to leave his bedroom

We knew that Parkinson's would
end our Grandfather
one day,
but not like this,
not this way

After the fire
we forgot about
our Grandfather
with his expressionless face
and his
slow-talking and slow-thinking,
about the way he involuntarily
magically blinked when we tapped him on his
forehead

He had become too slow
—our Grandfather
in the age of the iPhone, the iPad, the
iEverything

What we lost in the fire,
we found beneath that fake Van Gogh
painting,
(that had burned)
an original painting
(The Sower with Setting Sun)
that was worth millions

And we forgot our Grandfather even more

DOWN
BELOW

She tells me to pack the
parka with her,
she wants to wear it
down
there

It will be cold, she says
How can I make sure that I
won't freeze?
No one can take care of me
there

A shattering coldness suddenly crashes upon
me,
a cold—the coldest wind from Hades;
barking from a three-headed watchdog,
Cerberus,
as I feel him salivating for his next meal

No, it won't be cold, I calmly reply
You won't need the parka
You'll need shorts and skirts and sunglasses
because you'll be going up there
where it will be a perennial
summer
with gorgeous jasmine flowers and cherry
blossoms
and beautiful sunsets every
evening
and meals prepared for you every day for
life

But, no, she says
I'm preparing myself for
the death-cold hell below
Please place the parka on me
when I die
No one can take care of me
down
below

as I sense the dog sharpen his
canine teeth and salivate more

Lost Robot

He's lost,
the robot,
as he approaches the
passersby to find his
way back home

The husband and wife employed him as a
maintenance man
more than a year ago
but never programmed him to
find his way back home

They wanted to keep him there
and figured that he would never
want to leave

He had it too good,
they thought,
a comfortable bed to prevent
his metallic parts from becoming unhinged
and plenty of oil to smooth any heartaches

But the robot left one day
and became lost
and although the passersby told him
how to get back home
he never returned

FAILED ENCOUNTERS AT NEIMAN MARCUS

#1 With charred face and neck and melted lips and eyes, she sits in the back entrance

#2 . . . laughs and laughs just and her ignores she and, PETA with affiliated is she

of Neiman Marcus, knitting a scarf in the
dead of summer, and no one sees her, or if

whether know to wanting, her approaches
customer a when laughing still is and,

they see her, they pretend that they don't or
don't care either way, because

magazine Interview of issue latest the reading
while friends her with laughs and, it

she is another homeless in the City in the Hills
where white wings flutter and the Sirens

burning and coat mink ersatz an up holding by
this demonstrates and, animals to cruelty

sing their classical fugue and the sun shines
brighter and love is just a four letter word

decrying, sign a carrying while Fire Arcade
to listens and ears her in buds white the

and time will never wait for you when you
need it most . . .

places and iPod her on turns, Marcus Neiman
of entrance front the in sits she, them of army
an With

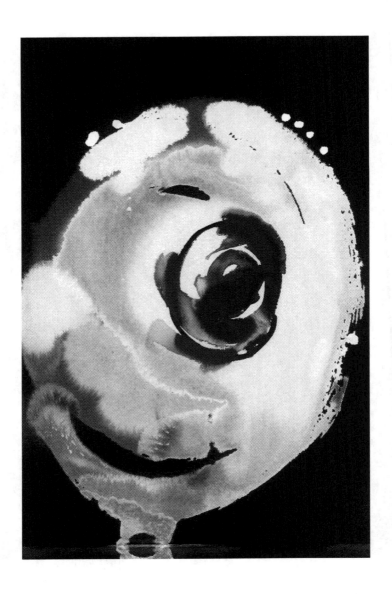

PART II:

HEART FAILURES

BLACK ANGEL

Black Angel
robs the clerk at
the convenience store
donning a Jackie-O mask
and brandishing a white revolver
with a few matches in her hand

Black Angel still wears the serrated black
wings
that she has so desperately
tried to cleave off
with a pair of pinking shears

Black Angel doesn't demand money
but simply some gasoline
to get these goddamn things
off her,
some Freedom and Justice from the wings
that have held her down for so long

The convenience clerk
understands this,
hands Black Angel the gasoline
and sees her douse it over the wings
and light them up
and watches that Jackie-O mask
melt in flames
while those black wings
flap proudly in the fire

THE CHILL OF OCTOBER

In a call center,
the chill of October
presses against the neck of the telemarketer
who sits in her cubicle
amid the Xerox machines and hundreds of
telephones
as she tries to sell whatever they tell her to
sell

Today, it's bottles of anti-aging pills
as she tries to muster the strength
to sell these capsules,
to "make it work," as they so often tell her,
although she realizes that everything ages
and dies
faster these days

In this dreary town in Michigan
she grabs on to her synthetic scarf
takes an extended-release Xanax tablet
to feel that something is protecting her
from the chill of this office,
from the chill of this northern town,
from the chill of October

She knows that her time is up,
that she'll soon be replaced by a recorded
message

She calls a home in California
(and dreams of being there,
recalling the sunny weather and her dog
before her parents divorced and she left home
for good)

Before she has a chance to speak to anyone,
the person on the other end
(whom she wants to so badly make a
connection with
and talk about California and the weather and
the roller coasters at Magic Mountain)
slams the phone on her
again

The Silence in TV

The silence surrounding them is palpable
as they watch TV
with its Dolby Stereo Surround
that clearly resonates
the actors' voices through a perfect
liquid crystal display

They can't say what they want to say,
the mother and daughter,
while the actors
say what the mother and daughter
have longed to say to each other
since the beginning

The TV characters speak for them:
The TV daughter says to her TV mom
—I have always loved you
while the TV mom emits her last sigh
in some hospital bed
and dies before she can say a thing
to her TV daughter

Heart Failed in the Back of a Taxi

Heart failed in the back of a taxi
on 51st and Park Ave.
in front of the Waldorf
as Death told him that she would no longer
be seeing him

She wore a fiery red lipstick,
Death did,
and a black spaghetti strapless
that shimmied about
every time she moved

He loved her,
he said,
and couldn't imagine life without her
especially in such a cold winter
when his Manhattan apartment felt
like hell,
too confined, too cold, and too lonely for any
kind of decent living

She didn't love him,
she said,
and there could never be a future together
They had a one-night stand
that's all
and she could never be his lover
Never
as she slammed the door of the taxi

At that moment,
at 11:11 pm,
in front of the gilded doors of the Waldorf,
in the back of a taxi,
his heart failed
and he was united with his love,
Death,
forever

TRASH

It was on that day in Tokyo
cloud and rain
mixed so much with that trash
of the landfill

We had gone
on a trip to see the
waste that was proliferating

it was growing legs
now   from
a   line
of Sapporo cans—
    the
    outline
    of
    the
    torso
    was
    being
    defined
    by boxes
    of   those
Pocky   Sticks—
its   head
was   inflating
dis   proportionately
by   crumpled pieces of
the   *Asahi Shimbun*—
it   had no arms

But the real trash was being
swept away into those crowded
Shinjuku streets

Masses huddled around one another
grimy faces with vacant stares,
palms held out for a sliver of yen,
that looked beyond one
to a better future

of trash that could
one day not
feel and think and remember
itself as
trash

STEAM ROOM

I don the white, pristine, terry-cloth robe
that the attendant offers me
at the prestigious fitness club

Yet, he offers me no advice

I enter a foggy quarter,
clouds of white
swarming the elderly men
huddled around one another
hoping to sweat
pounds, worries,
guilt

Their robes are coming undone
as more steam douses them
bellies of white, creased thighs,
striae,
now grossly
visible

I hold tightly onto my robe
fearing evaporation into a
weightless air,
into the confluence of extra appendage
in this room

as in a gas chamber
masses pressed,
masses condensed together
in Dacau, Nuremberg, Auschwitz
sensing these vapors,
genocidal molecules,
crawling their way to them and
into them
as they become indistinguishable
from another
as corpses, Muselman, faces of death

But that attendant had
offered me no advice

CAMERA LUCIDA

Of course, it is so clear now
you were pointing to this even back then
(if I hadn't looked so closely, I would've seen)

With those burnished edges and lacquered
black-and-white veneer
you were pointing, gesturing
that this will all end one day
(sooner than I'd like)

Your gaze captured meticulously,
instantaneously,
what had taken so long to develop

Mother with her Twiggy haircut
lavished in Pucci
eyes somewhat downcast and lacklustered
nevertheless smiling for you, for me
(however reticently)
as I tried to blow the birthday candles
thinking that this will be hard, so much
harder
next year

But you knew (with your Sibylesque eyes)
that the arduous task was yet to come,
that I had not gone far enough,
that I would be scavenging details all these
years
without knowing the purpose you served

Years and years have wasted
As you and I have become wizened,
(my hair harrowingly white and shorn)
the function you served is now so lucid

Mother has since passed
Yet you captured that moment,
that instant that thwarted death,
while death was sitting with her,
with us,
was us,
gazing at you sheepishly,
whispering to us,
—pose like this**

**   "To the memory of my grandmother, Malak Tehrani"

DEATH & CO.

They called again last night,
Derrida and Heidegger,
via spectral telephony
to alert me
that the landline
had not been
working

They had tried it
the night before last
only to be surprised by the voice
on the other end

Not mine,
they said,
a counterfeit to be sure,
but not my voice:
they needed to alert me

Where once crisp, voices now muffled,
those of Jacques and Martin,
so I questioned their authenticity
(a "Heidegger" had, apparently, done this to
Derrida before)

Incoherent babble now
mixed with so much static
that before they could respond,
an aborted, spectral telephony

I needed to alert *them*

On the other end

THE (MODERN) TRIAL

The housekeeper,
M.,
cleans the corners and
crevices of that disgusting
bathroom
in the sullied
motel room
meticulously,
mathematically,
as if her life depended on
it

The dirt makes her feel like the
colorful immigrant they tell her she is,
always on trial to prove her citizenship—
on trial as an ungrateful thief

There is disgust in this bathroom:
urine
spit
blood
dirt

She cleans it all,
cleans herself,
with caustic bleach
burning her hands
everyday

She doesn't mind,
it's a ritual,
a way to be free
when she's constantly on
trial for being
shit

PART III:

HEART MURMURS

HONEY'S GONE

This "Busy Bee" honey bottle
in the form of a plastic bear
is motionless, static
has no busi-ness about it

Yet it contains the honey
that supplies me
with the sweetest nourishment
sticky, congealed
but almost gone

I cannot see the bees
that have made this honey
on which I feast
they whose work goes unrecognized
that remain anonymous
and sustain me

The plastic bear
stares at me
black dots for beady eyes and snout
its gaze is suppliant and far-reaching
seeming to say in its silence:
I, too, have supplied you,
molded in plastic
in the factory
in the shape of this bear,
I had no choice
but to work for you
Please recognize my
Importance

But I have no use for it
anymore
The sweet honey's gone
and the bear is thrown in with the
rubbish

TURK KAHVESI

I'm a fortune-teller
of Turkish origin
who reads the
grooves and outlines of
coffee that you've
drunk

Drink the heavy kahve, slowly
Turn the cup over into the saucer, quickly
and from the thick layer of dregs
at the bottom of the cup
I'll give you an idea of
your future

(You turn the cup over)

I see a beast
with three heads
and eight arms
and fire behind the beast that beckons it
forward

one head: Medusa's
two: Athena's
three: yours

You will live 38 more years
and find unrequited, burning love
exactly
three times
and meet your demise
organically, on soil of your
origin

The kahve does not lie
It has nothing at stake
It has wasted its life
to give you an indication of
yours
I'm simply a medium,
a fortune-teller of meager means

(You look inside the ornate cup
and see a thick layer of sludgy grounds,
evidence of a life lived,
not of anything to come)

You and the kahve have both been
drunk,
wasted

Love Ho(tel)

In Kanagawa prefecture
in Japan
in a love ho(tel)
named Spellworks
the eager lovers
select their room
fast
too fast
so as to detract
attention
from themselves

Like a vending machine,
the rooms and corresponding
prices are displayed
and ready for the taking
with the push of a
button

Reflexively,
fast,
too fast,
he pushes and selects
Cleopatra's Spell,
a room with a queen-sized bed
and smell of Mediterranean spice
all for 8000 ¥
so cheap

So cheap
their encounter will be,
though she is not a
prostitute but a
respectable woman
from a middle-class
family in Yokohama

[The ho(tel) staff
doesn't look,
has never looked
for fear of being
looked and perceived
as filth that runs this shitty
place, this love ho(tel)]

The plastic card,
the key to Cleopatra's Spell
is dispensed
into the machine
and he takes it into
his sweaty palms,
glances furtively at his lover,
takes her left hand,
and leads her upstairs,
to work his magic
in the dark

LIKE ICARUS

In Oia,
amid the sunset
with houses cobalt blue and white
and the throng of those Europeans
with their polyglot tongues,
she feels lost

The American,
a tourist on vacation
in Santorini,
she feels the gaze of the
group scorching her
like the Greek sun
and like Icarus
crush her to the ground

She thinks that those Europeans
the French, Germans, and Spaniards
are ridiculing, mocking her
from behind

She presses her necklace
emblazoned with the US flag
the red, white, and blue
against her chest
It comforts her
among the souvlaki and tzatziki
for which she has no palate

A shopkeeper of a store,
lined along the narrow cobble-stone street,
motions for her to enter

Reluctantly, she does so
and the shopkeeper
a Greek with the bluest
eye and the whitest skin
hands her a necklace
with a single eye strewn
about the thinnest black string

You must wear this
she says
you need this,
Mati,
a good eye to
replace and vanquish
the evil eye of Others

The tourist instinctively rips the
necklace of red, white, and blue
and throws it on the floor
and replaces it with the
single eye, the
apotropaic talisman
of light and dark blue
and white

Mati,
the shopkeeper repeats
wear it close,
keep it close

The American presses the single eye
against her breast
and
departs the store hurriedly
wanting to catch the sunset
not realizing that this
thinnest black string
that holds the eye,
the *Mati*,
has ripped and been thrown into
the street
and crushed by the footsteps
of the heavy German
who reeks of strong ouzo
and pungent body odor

TIGHTER

He likes to wear
his watch
tight
so tight
and feel his hand
throb,
see the hand
slowly turn
blue

Like manacles,
the tight-fitting watch
makes him feel
like the prisoner that
he is—
always already
having surrendered—
always already
in control
of how he wants things
to end

He removes another link
from the metallic strap
and tightens the watch
even more

DEEPER CUTS

With a few needles and syringes
she changes her face
several times a month
and lets the anesthesia
talk for her

Restylane, Juviderm, Botox, Radiesse
they are her friends now,
her confidants,
that won't reveal
how she killed her old
face
(in the dead of night, with deep cuts)
and buried it alive

The primordial face is
still there
imprisoned
by volumizing fillers
and botulinum toxins
that hold it
hostage in the
open grave

At Malpensa Airport,
in Milan,
she is detained
by the customs officer:
—Signora, the face doesn't match the
passport photo

She takes out her smoking gun,
that old knife,
and begins to cut her face
deeper and deeper
below the Restylane and Radiesse
until the old one emerges:
a face
short of breath, a little
blue, gasping for air
as she grabs it by the
hollow, shrunken cheeks and says to the
officer:
—You mean this pathetic thing? It died
before it was ever born

CAESURA

There's something here
in the walls—
I hear it

Perhaps it's just a squirrel
looking for nuts and seeds
that has managed to find a passageway
to the house,
its walls

But it's louder,
like the sound of a hacksaw
cutting wood

Sometimes it sounds like
the guttural shout of
wild horses,
trapped,
vehemently kicking from
the inside

And then it's quiet.

It all abruptly stops,
like a heart
that has worked so hard
and then given up
on life—
when it beat so
forcefully, so
vigorously
all the days
before